SHORT WALKS
NORFOLK
BROADS AND COAST

by Laurence Mitchell

Approaching Burnham Overy Mill (Walk 8)

CONTENTS

Using this guide... 4
Route summary table 6
Map key 7
Introduction... 9
   Walking in Norfolk 10
   What to see 11
   Travel 11
   Where to stay.. 11

The walks
   1.   Horsey Mere and Horsey Gap 13
   2.   Happisburgh to Ostend 19
   3.   Cromer to Overstrand 23
   4.   Sheringham and West Runton 29
   5.   Cley next the Sea... 33
   6.   Blakeney and Blakeney Downs...................................... 37
   7.   Wells-next-the-Sea and Holkham 41
   8.   Burnham Deepdale to Burnham Overy Staithe..................... 47
   9.   Thornham and Holme-next-the-Sea........................... 55
   10. Sandringham Royal Parkland... 61
   11. Historic Norwich 65
   12. Whitlingham Country Park 71
   13. Great Yarmouth.. 75
   14. Womack Water and Horse Fen 81
   15. Upton Dyke... 87

Useful information 94

USING THIS GUIDE

Routes in this book

In this book you will find a selection of easy or moderate walks suitable for almost everyone, including casual walkers and families with children, or for when you only have a short time to fill. The routes have been carefully chosen to allow you to explore the area and its attractions. Most routes are circular or out-and-back, although some linear walks may be included that use public transport to get back to the start. Although there may be some climbs there is no challenging terrain, but do bear in mind that conditions can sometimes be wet or muddy underfoot. A route summary table is included on page 6 to help you choose the right walk.

Clothing and footwear

You won't need any special equipment to enjoy these walks. The weather in Britain can be changeable, so choose clothing suitable for the season and wear or carry a waterproof jacket. For footwear, comfortable walking boots or trainers with a good grip are best. A small rucksack for drinks, snacks and spare clothing is useful. See www.adventuresmart.uk.

Walk descriptions

At the beginning of each walk you'll find all the information you need:

- start/finish location, with a what3words address to help you find it
- parking and transport information, estimated walking time, total distance and climb
- details of public toilets available along the route and where you can get refreshments
- a summary of the key highlights of the walk and what you might see

Timings given are the time to complete the walk at a reasonable walking pace. Allow extra time for extended stops or if walking with children.

The route is described in clear, easy-to-follow directions, with each waypoint marked on an accompanying map extract. It's a good idea to read the whole of the route instructions before setting out, so that you know what to expect.

Maps, GPX files and what3words

Extracts from the OS® 1:25,000 map accompany each route. GPX files for all the walks in this book are available to download at www.cicerone.co.uk/1245/gpx.

What3words is a free smartphone app which identifies every 3m square of the globe with a unique three-word address, e.g. ///destiny.cafe.sonic. For more information see https://what3words.com/products/what3words-app.

USING THIS GUIDE

Walking with children

Even young children can be surprisingly strong walkers, but every family is different and you may need to adapt the timings given in this book to take that into account. Make sure you go at the pace of the slowest member and choose a walk with an exciting objective in mind, such as a cave, river, waterfall or picnic spot. Many of the walks can be shortened to suit – suggestions are included at the end of the route description.

Dogs

Sheep or cattle may be found grazing on a number of these walks. Keep dogs under control at all times so that they don't scare or disturb livestock or wildlife. Cattle, particularly cows with calves, may very occasionally pose a risk to walkers with dogs. If you ever feel threatened by cattle, you should let go of your dog's lead and let it run free.

Enjoying the countryside responsibly

Enjoy the countryside and treat it with respect to protect our natural environments. Stick to footpaths and take your litter home with you. When driving, slow down on rural roads and park considerately, or better still use public transport. For more details check out www.gov.uk/countryside-code.

The Countryside Code

Respect everyone
- be considerate to those living in, working in and enjoying the countryside
- leave gates and property as you find them
- do not block access to gateways or driveways when parking
- be nice, say hello, share the space
- follow local signs and keep to marked paths unless wider access is available

Protect the environment
- take your litter home – leave no trace of your visit
- do not light fires and only have BBQs where signs say you can
- always keep dogs under control and in sight
- dog poo – bag it and bin it – any public waste bin will do
- care for nature – do not cause damage or disturbance

Enjoy the outdoors
- check your route and local conditions
- plan your adventure – know what to expect and what you can do
- enjoy your visit, have fun, make a memory

ROUTE SUMMARY TABLE

WALK NAME	START POINT	TIME	DISTANCE
1. Horsey Mere and Horsey Gap	Horsey Windpump	2hr 30min	8km (5 miles)
2. Happisburgh to Ostend	Happisburgh beach car park	1hr 30min	5.2km (3.2 miles)
3. Cromer to Overstrand	Cromer Pier	2hr 30min	7km (4.3 miles)
4. Sheringham and West Runton	Clock Tower, Sheringham	2hr	6.2km (3.9 miles)
5. Cley next the Sea	Cley Marshes nature reserve	2hr	5.9km (3.7 miles)
6. Blakeney and Blakeney Downs	Blakeney village sign	1hr 30min	5.3km (3.3 miles)
7. Wells-next-the-Sea and Holkham	Wells-next-the-Sea	3hr	10km (6.2 miles)
8. Burnham Deepdale to Burnham Overy Staithe	Burnham Deepdale	2hr	6.5km (4 miles)
9. Thornham and Holme-next-the-Sea	St Mary's Church, Thornham	3hr 30min	10.7km (6.6 miles)
10. Sandringham Royal Parkland	The Courtyard, Sandringham	1hr 30min	4.5km (2.8 miles)
11. Historic Norwich	The Forum, Norwich	1hr 30min	4.4km (2.7 miles)
12. Whitlingham Country Park	Whitlingham Great Broad	2hr	6.2km (3.9 miles)
13. Great Yarmouth	Great Yarmouth Minster	2hr	5.9km (3.7 miles)
14. Womack Water and Horse Fen	Womack Staithe, Ludham	1hr 45min	5.3km (3.3 miles)
15. Upton Dyke	Upton Dyke	1hr 30min	4.6km (2.9 miles)

ROUTE SUMMARY TABLE

HIGHLIGHTS
Reedbeds, dunes, beach, seals (in winter)
Coastal scenery, historic church, cliffs
Beach, clifftop views, coastal town
Sea views, beach, coastal resort
Shingle bank, nature reserve, attractive village
Attractive coastal village, saltmarsh, farmland
Coastal resort, pine woodland, beach, estate parkland
Saltmarsh, mudflats, sailing harbour
Sand dunes, beach, pretty villages
Park woodland
Medieval buildings, history, river walk
Waterside walk, woodland
Historic buildings, town walls
Broads scenery, river views
Windmills, fen, village

SYMBOLS USED ON ROUTE MAPS

S — Start point

F — Finish point

SF — Start and finish at the same place

4→ — Waypoint

〜 — Route line

MAPPING IS SHOWN AT A SCALE OF 1:25,000

```
0 KM      0.25      0.5
|----|----|----|----|
0 miles       0.25
```

DOWNLOAD THE GPX FILES FOR FREE AT
www.cicerone.co.uk/1245/gpx

Happisburgh's iconic lighthouse (Walk 2)

INTRODUCTION

A dramatic cliffhanger at Happisburgh (Walk 2)

As a county, Norfolk has some very distinctive landscapes to its name. Nowhere is this more apparent than along its coastline, which stretches from King's Lynn in the west to just south of Great Yarmouth in the east. The Norfolk coast has been popular with visitors since Victorian times, when the introduction of railways gave easy access to the resorts of Cromer, Sheringham and Hunstanton. These days, most people tend to arrive by car although the appeal of the Norfolk coastline, with its unique combination of beaches, saltmarsh, shingle and tidal creeks, is undiminished.

Norfolk is also home to a unique patchwork of lakes and rivers known as the Broads, which lies a little way inland from the county's northeast coast. While many come here for boating holidays in summer, the area also offers some excellent walking. Although appearances may be deceptive, the Norfolk Broads are not naturally formed but man-made; the result of extensive flooding of areas where peat-digging took place in the medieval period. With reed beds and waterways providing valuable habitat for a number of specialist plants, birds and insects, the Broads National Park is Britain's largest protected wetland.

SHORT WALKS NORFOLK

Colegate in Norwich has many fine buildings as well as two medieval churches (Walk 11)

Walking in Norfolk

With few serious hills to contend with, walking in Norfolk is on the whole undemanding. That is not to say it is uninteresting, as it is surprisingly variable, especially along the county's coastline, which changes character considerably as you travel either east or west from Cromer and Sheringham, the resorts that lie at its central point.

West of Sheringham is a region composed largely of saltmarsh and muddy tidal inlets interspersed with expanses of pristine sand like that at Holkham. With several small, protected harbours, it is a stretch of coast that is especially popular with weekend sailors, while its mudflats and marshes provide shelter for a wide variety of nesting and migrating birds. Such landscapes can be seen to good advantage at Burnham Overy Staithe (Walk 8), Cley next the Sea (Walk 5) and Thornham (Walk 9). In contrast, east of Cromer, as far as the Suffolk border, is a coastal strip that is largely made up of sandy beaches backed by dunes or low cliffs. This northeast coastline is often victim to savage coastal erosion, a phenomenon that can be readily appreciated at villages like Happisburgh (Walk 2).

Venturing a little way inland, walks 14 and 15 give a flavour of the unique scenery that the Norfolk Broads has to offer. Walk 1 offers a mixture of broad and coast, taking in both landscapes along the way. With the exception of Walk 8, which could be done as either linear or there-and-back, all of the walks offered in this book are circular.

What to see

Although it is tempting to focus solely on the coast or the Broads, the city of Norwich should not be overlooked on any visit to Norfolk. For centuries the second largest city in England, Norwich has a wealth of medieval churches within its city walls, as well as the alleyways and courtyards that constitute the pedestrianised Lanes. Norwich is also home to a fine Norman castle and cathedral and one of the oldest marketplaces in the country. The River Wensum that runs through the heart of the city is a reminder that Norwich was once firmly connected by trade to the coast at Great Yarmouth, which lies only 20 or so miles distant. Great Yarmouth itself, despite having the modern-day appearance of a traditional, perhaps slightly old-fashioned, holiday resort, is another place with a rich and varied history, having a long-standing seafaring tradition and the second most complete medieval town walls in the country.

Travel

Both Cromer and Sheringham are connected to Norwich by rail and bus, which in turn has regular rail services to London and the Midlands. Great Yarmouth, too, has regular bus and train connections to Norwich. The coast between Sheringham and Wells-next-the-Sea is well served by the regular Coasthopper CH1 bus service, which can be used to reach the start and end points of several walks in this book. This connects in Wells-next-the-Sea with the Coastliner 36 service, which runs west along the coast to King's Lynn via Hunstanton, passing Sandringham along the way. Both services run hourly through the day.

In a few cases, in particular those in the Broads, the start point of a walk is easier to reach by using your own transport, although even here there is usually a bus service that passes relatively close by.

Where to stay

There is a wide variety of accommodation in the area that ranges from campsites to B&Bs, rental cottages, smart hotels and even glamping. Wells-next-the-Sea, Blakeney and Cromer all make good bases for staying on the coast, although in summer it is best to book well ahead.

Brograve Drainage Mill was built in 1771

WALK 1
Horsey Mere and Horsey Gap

Start/finish	Horsey Windpump
Locate	///reading.refreshed.situates
Cafes/pubs	Pub in Horsey, cafes at Horsey Windpump and Horsey Corner
Transport	No public transport
Parking	Pay & display car park at Horsey Windpump (NR29 4EE)
Toilets	In car park

Time 2hr 30min
Distance 8km (5 miles)
Climb 0m

Featuring an outlying broad and a sandy stretch of Norfolk coastline, this is an enjoyable walk at any time of year

This route begins and ends at the windmill next to Horsey Mere, a small isolated broad close to the coast. After winding past reedbeds and grazing meadows, it reaches the coast at Horsey Gap, a place well-known for its large colony of grey seals. From Horsey Gap the route traces the line of dunes south for a while before following quiet tracks across country to return to the start.

Horsey Windpump and boats at Staithe

Following the path around Horsey Mere

1 Leaving the car park take the track that leads west along the staithe away from the windpump. This soon turns sharp right to skirt around **Horsey Mere** (the water itself is mostly obscured by the extensive reedbeds). Horsey Mere, owned, like the windpump, by the National Trust, is one of the most northerly of the Norfolk Broads. Continue past open fields on the right and a fence on the left to reach the channel of **Waxham New Cut**.

2 Follow the path along the channel to arrive at the ruined but picturesque **Brograve Drainage Mill** on the opposite bank.

The Brograve Drainage Mill, a Grade 2 listed building, was built in 1771 by Sir Berney Brograve. Originally constructed to drain water from the Brograve Levels, it is thought to have been functional until around 1930.

WALK 1 – HORSEY MERE AND HORSEY GAP

3 Turn right to follow the track between fields. On reaching a wood, turn left then right towards a row of houses ahead. At the lane in front of the houses, go right then immediately left along the signed path. This follows a hedge that leads to a T-junction of paths. Go left here to follow a field boundary to the road.

4 Turn right at the road then, at the next corner, take the lane to the left, signed for Horsey Gap car park. The area around the car park can become very busy in winter, especially around Christmas and New Year, when many come to view the grey seals on the beach here.

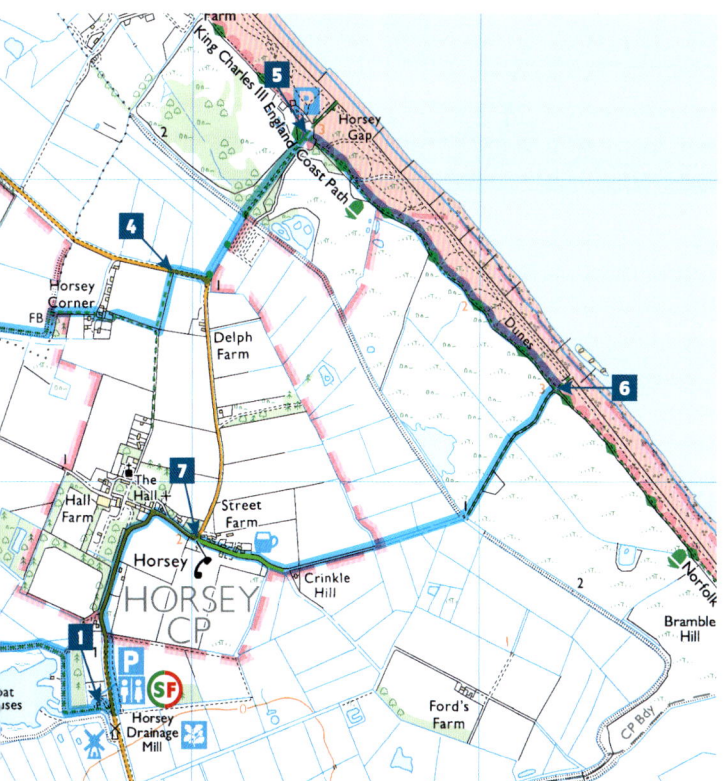

A kestrel on a fence post behind the dunes at Horsey Gap

5 Arriving at the **car park**, take the signed Norfolk Coast Path to the right. This leads behind the dunes, from where a World War 2 pillbox can be seen to the left. Continue to reach a path to the right alongside another Norfolk Coast Path sign that says: 'Nelson Head 1 mile.'

6 Go right, heading inland. The path widens to become a farm track before joining a minor road by a cottage. Turn right to pass the **Nelson Head pub** before arriving at a junction.

7 Turn left, then take the permissive path that follows a field edge alongside the road. This re-emerges to become a narrow path next to the road itself before going back through a gap and along a hedge to arrive at a gate opposite the cafe and windpump **car park**. Go through the gate, then cross the road to return to the start.

> **— To shorten**
> Rather than continuing to the beach and dunes, turn right at the T-junction of footpaths just before Waypoint 4. This leads back to Horsey village and the junction at Waypoint 7, shortening the walk by about 3km (1hr).

WALK 1 – HORSEY MERE AND HORSEY GAP

Grey seals at Horsey

Horsey Gap is home to one of the largest colonies of grey seals in England. Numbers have increased in recent years to more than 3,500 pups being born in the 2023/2024 season. Although the seals can be seen here on the beach year-round, the pupping season is from late October to February. At this time of year they should only be observed at distance from the viewing platforms in the dunes. Dogs, of course, should also be kept under full control.

The Nelson Head pub, Horsey village

St Mary's Church, Happisburgh, has the second highest tower in Norfolk

WALK 2
Happisburgh to Ostend

Time 1hr 30min
Distance 5.2km (3.2 miles)
Climb 35m

A short clifftop walk that gives a taste of the challenges that face this dramatically eroding coastline

Start/finish	Happisburgh beach car park
Locate	///toasters.navigate.glass
Cafes/pubs	Pub in Happisburgh
Transport	Buses from Stalham, Mundesley and North Walsham
Parking	Happisburgh pay & display car park (N12 0PR)
Toilets	In car park

This walk takes in the crumbling cliffs of northeast Norfolk's dynamic coastline, as well as the historic sights of this erosion-threatened village. While Happisburgh, pronounced 'Haze-bruh', continues to do battle with the North Sea, its historic St Mary's church and iconic red-banded lighthouse still stand proudly…for the time being! Both structures are important landmarks for this part of the coast.

Approaching Happisburgh from Ostend, St Mary's Church in the distance

SHORT WALKS NORFOLK

1 Leaving the car park, turn away from the beach to walk along Beach Road a short distance to arrive at a junction where a signed footpath leads to the right across a field. After going through a gate, head along the path that curves left towards St Mary's Church and continue in the same direction to reach a Norfolk Coast Path signpost close to the cliff edge.

The effects of the severe erosion, typical of this coast, can be seen clearly here. Until recently, a caravan park used to top the cliffs here but with continued relentless erosion it had to be abandoned.

2 Turn left and follow the coast path to reach a pair of concrete bunkers where a farm track leads inland.

WALK 2 – HAPPISBURGH TO OSTEND

Eroding cliffs and the beach at Happisburgh

3 With distant views of the gas terminal of Bacton ahead, ignore the farm track inland to continue along the coast path until reaching a row of bungalows at the edge of **Ostend** village. In 2002 a Cuvier's beaked whale, a deep-sea whale rarely seen in offshore waters, was stranded on Ostend beach.

4 Walk past the bungalows before turning left at the road. Continue past a junction to the right then turn left at a signed footpath that leads back in the direction of Happisburgh. Soon, arriving at a track, go right to follow the footpath along field edges until reaching a farm track next to some isolated houses.

The field footpath may be quite overgrown in late summer. An alternative is to turn left and retrace steps along the coast path. The route can then be rejoined by turning right along the farm track by the concrete bunkers.

5 Bear right along the farm track to **Church Farm** where the track becomes a road. Continue straight ahead past the Wenn Evans Centre on the right before arriving at the gate of **St Mary's Church**.

St Mary's has the second highest church tower in Norfolk. The churchyard has a mound that contains the remains of 119 sailors from HMS Invincible, which sank in a storm here in 1801 while on its way to join Nelson's fleet.

Happisburgh village sign and High Street

6 From the church gate, walk down Church Street to reach The Street. The village pub, the Hill House Inn, is set back a little way above The Street to the left. Go down The Street to arrive at a junction with Beach Road on the left. Turn left and follow Beach Road to the end to return to the start point.

– To shorten

This walk could be shortened by about 2km (40min) by turning left along the farm track at the concrete bunkers at Waypoint 3. The route would then be rejoined on reaching the farm track that leads to Church Farm.

Ancient footsteps at Happisburgh

Happisburgh beach has revealed evidence of the earliest human occupation of Britain: the oldest human footprints in Europe, around 900,000 years old, were discovered preserved in mud in 2013; and a beautifully preserved 800,000-year-old flint hand-axe was found protruding from a cliff by a dog-walker in 2000. Both are believed to have been left by *Homo antecessor*, a long-extinct early human species that could have roamed this region when Britain was still attached to the European mainland.

WALK 3
Cromer to Overstrand

Start/finish	*Cromer Pier*
Locate	*///unhelpful.struck.openings*
Cafes/pubs	*Cafes and pubs in Cromer, cafe and pub in Overstrand*
Transport	*Train and buses to Cromer*
Parking	*Pay & display car parks on Meadow Road (NR27 9DS) and Runton Road (NR27 9AU)*
Toilets	*Cromer Pier and RNLI Museum*

Time 2hr 30min
Distance 7km (4.3 miles)
Climb 130m

A scenic walk between two popular resorts that offers sweeping views along the north Norfolk coast

This varied walk between two coastal resorts stays close to the sea all the way. It follows the beach to Overstrand before returning to Cromer along a cliff-top route that gives excellent views of the Norfolk coastline and Cromer's iconic pier. There is also the option of stopping for a swim or a paddle on the outgoing leg.

RNLI Museum and St Peter & St Paul Church, Cromer

SHORT WALKS NORFOLK

1 Facing the entrance to Cromer Pier, go right along the esplanade until reaching a concrete ramp next to the Rocket House cafe and the **RNLI Museum**.

> The RNLI Henry Blogg Museum is dedicated to the history of Cromer's lifeboats and Henry Blogg, who served as coxswain for 53 years. Together with his crew, he saved a total of 873 lives from the North Sea.

2 Continue along the gangway beyond the cafe and museum towards the beach huts ahead, passing the tractors and fishing boats used by Cromer's crab fleet. At the end of the beach huts, depending on the state of the tide, you can either follow the concrete path close to the cliffs or walk along the beach itself past a series of wooden **groynes** (breakwaters). Continue for about 1.5km until you arrive at the concrete ramp and steps that lead up to **Overstrand**.

Poppies on the clifftop walk between Cromer and Overstrand

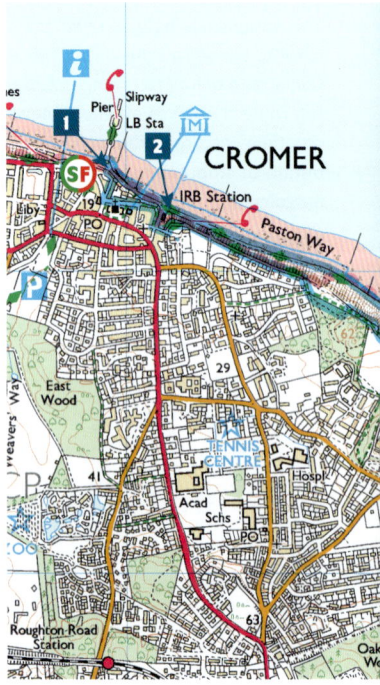

WALK 3 – CROMER TO OVERSTRAND

Herring gulls on a groyne at Cromer Beach

3 Go up the ramp and steps to head uphill to reach a Norfolk Coast Path signpost close to a car park. Turn right and go through the car park towards a flagpole, where a gate leads to a permissive path close to the cliff. Follow this to emerge at a **golf course** where the path climbs gently through gorse and bracken. At the top of the rise, where there is a bench, a white lighthouse comes into view to the left.

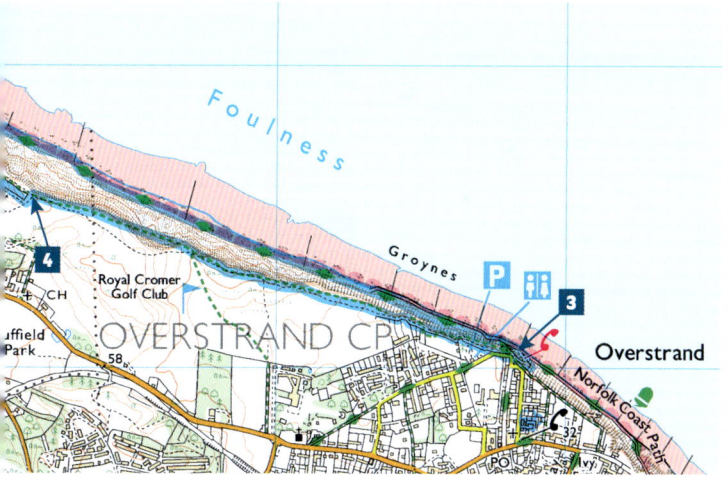

The clifftop path between Overstrand and Cromer

Overstrand, a small resort that was once known as 'the village of millionaires' because of its popularity with the Victorian upper classes, has many grand buildings that date from the turn of the 20th century.

4 From the bench take the path downhill, which leads to a broad area of gorse where several paths converge. Continue in the same direction to follow a broad gravel path past a recreation ground. The path continues past houses and North Lodge Park. Reaching a small park in a dip, go around this to head along East Street and then Tucker Street, which passes the **Church of St Peter & St Paul**. The church tower is the tallest in Norfolk, and peregrine falcons regularly nest upon it. Turn right on Jetty Street to arrive at the staggered walkway that leads back down to the pier.

✢ To lengthen

A short (1km) detour into Overstrand village can be made at Waypoint 3, walking up to the White Lion pub before turning right and right again to return via The Londs, a lane that has many attractive flint cottages.

WALK 3 – CROMER TO OVERSTRAND

The narrow but elegant Jetty Street at Cromer's seafront

Cromer Pier

Cromer Pier, which is home to the town's offshore lifeboat at its far end, is one of only five in the country that has a fully functioning theatre. Uniquely, it is the only one in the world that can still boast a full season end of pier show. Although records of a pier of sorts – more likely a jetty – date back to 1391, the current pier was opened to the public in 1902. The pier, which has free entry, is Grade 2 listed and 151m long, is popular as a place for children to go crabbing.

An elegant gateway with a nautical theme at Sheringham seafront

WALK 4
Sheringham and West Runton

Start/finish	Sheringham Clock Tower
Locate	///snacks.rear.walked
Cafes/pubs	Pubs and cafes in Sheringham and West Runton
Transport	Train to Norwich. Buses to Cromer and Wells-next-the-Sea
Parking	Station Approach pay & display car park (NR26 8RG)
Toilets	In car park and at West Runton slipway

Time 2hr
Distance 6.2km (3.9 miles)
Climb 120m

This coastal walk between two neighbouring seaside resorts offers coastal views and the option of a popular beach along the way

This walk connecting two popular coastal resorts begins in the centre of Sheringham, from where it visits the seafront before climbing gently to one of the county's rare highpoints further along the coast. From here, it descends to West Runton Beach with its excellent bathing and acclaimed prehistoric heritage. The return leg takes in a little of West Runton village before following a slightly more inland route back to Sheringham.

Beach huts line the promenade at Sheringham

1 Starting at the Clock Tower, walk along High Street to soon reach the seafront.

> ⓘ *Sheringham Clock Tower was originally built in 1862 as a water pump for the town. The clock was added in 1903.*

2 Turn right along the promenade to go past the Crown pub and down a few steps by **Sheringham Museum**. Continue past the jetty and beach, and along a line of beach huts until reaching a path, signed Norfolk Coast Path, that climbs up to the right. Follow this uphill to reach the top of the Beeston Hill, known locally as **Beeston Bump**, where there is a triangulation pillar.

> **Beeston Bump, 63m high, is an isolated part of the 14km-long Cromer Ridge, a ridge of glacial moraine deposited by retreating glaciers at the end of the last ice age.**

3 Continue along the path to descend the hill, passing an information board for Beeston Regis Nature Trail and a holiday park. The path passes in front of a **caravan site** before arriving at a car park. Go through the **car park** to reach the road that joins the slipway down to West Runton Beach, a short detour.

WALK 4 – SHERINGHAM AND WEST RUNTON

The short climb up Beeston Bump

The beach, which is popular with bathers, has a cafe with a gift shop and small museum halfway down the slipway.

4 Walking uphill from the slipway, follow **Water Lane** up to the main road where there is a pub garden. Turn right along Cromer Road and go past **Holy Trinity Church** and a war memorial, continuing in the same direction until reaching the railway line that passes beneath the road.

5 Take the footpath that runs parallel to the railway line to the right. This passes a meadow beneath Beeston Regis' All Saints Church before arriving

West Runton Beach with Cromer Pier in the distance

at a road with a railway crossing. Take the path to the right here that leads up to the houses beneath **Beeston Bump**. This soon merges into Nelson Road, which later joins Cliff Road. On reaching Beeston Road go left, then right, to soon arrive back at Sheringham High Street. Turn left to walk the short distance back to the start at the Clock Tower.

The West Runton Mammoth

The bones of the so-called West Runton Mammoth, discovered in the cliffs at West Runton in the 1990s, belong to the most complete mammoth skeleton ever found in Britain. They are also the oldest, being an estimated 600,000 to 700,000 years old, and belong to the Steppe mammoth species *Mammuthus trogontherii*. Twice the size of a modern African elephant, it would have weighed 10 tonnes and been around 4m tall. Initially just a single pelvic bone was discovered exposed in the cliffs in 1990, but a year later further bones were uncovered by winter storms. A major excavation followed in 1995.

WALK 5
Cley next the Sea

Start/finish	Cley Marshes nature reserve visitor centre
Locate	///overruns.swooned.roughness
Cafes/pubs	Cafe at visitor centre, cafes and pubs in Cley next the Sea
Transport	Coasthopper CH1 bus service from Cromer and Wells-next-the-Sea
Parking	Pay & display car park at visitor centre (NR25 7SA)
Toilets	In visitor centre

Time 2hr
Distance 5.9km (3.7 miles)
Climb 10m

A coastal walk that circuits a well-known nature reserve before winding through an attractive flint-built village

This delightful walk begins by circuiting part of the Cley Marshes nature reserve, a well-managed reserve widely acknowledged as one of the most rewarding places for birdwatching in the country. After following a high shingle bank along the shore to Cley Eye, the route leads inland past an iconic windmill and through the streets of Cley next the Sea, an attractive coastal village built largely of flint pebble, before returning to the visitor centre on the coast road.

The shingle beach at Cley Eye

SHORT WALKS NORFOLK

1 From the car park in front of the cafe and visitor centre cross the coast road then turn right along the footpath that runs parallel to it. Follow this along the edge of **Cley Marshes nature reserve** to reach a small **car park**.

2 Go through the gate to follow the raised path that leads left away from the road to reach the shingle bank ahead.

Cley Marshes nature reserve was purchased by the Norfolk Wildlife Trust in 1926 to be held 'in perpetuity as a breeding bird sanctuary'. As well as having many breeding birds, especially waders, it also receives many rare vagrants on passage.

Cley Windmill and channel of the River Glaven

3 From the shingle bank, head left with the sea on your right. If the tide is out it may be easier to walk along

Heading towards the shingle bank

the sand for this part of the route. Follow the shingle bank as far as the **car park** at Cley Eye. Go through the car park and cross the road to reach a path that leads left along a raised bank inland towards Cley village.

4 Follow the raised path alongside the coast road. The path veers right then leaves the coast road. Continue along the path to reach **Cley Windmill**.

Cley Windmill was built in the early 19th century and was a working windmill until the 1920s when its new owner converted it into a holiday home. The five-storey mill is now a guesthouse with B&B and self-catering accommodation.

5 From the windmill, continue past moored boats along a channel of the River Glaven. The Glaven, which is

SHORT WALKS NORFOLK

17km long and rises inland close to Bodham, is a rare chalk stream, one of 160 found in the UK. The path continues as a raised path alongside reedbeds before arriving at steps down to New Road.

6 Go down the steps and turn left along the road to reach a T-junction. Turn left at the T-junction. Soon after, go right at a telephone box, along the narrow pathway that runs between flint cottages to reach a lane. Turn left here to soon rejoin High Street. Turn right along the street and at the end of the village continue along the signed footpath that runs parallel to the coast road to soon arrive back at the **visitor centre** and starting point.

Cley Windmill, an iconic landmark, is now used for holiday lettings

— To shorten

To shorten the walk by about 1km, turn left at Cley Windmill (Waypoint 5) to join High Street. Turn left again to follow the road to the visitor centre.

Cley next the Sea

The village of Cley is no longer quite as 'next the sea' as it used to be. In the medieval period Cley was a prosperous port exporting grain, cloth and malt, and there was a busy harbour right next to where St Margaret's Church now stands. Some of the village architecture, in particular its Flemish gables, serve as a reminder of Cley's former trade with the Low Countries. The port went into serious decline in the 17th century when its harbour began silting up, largely the result of ambitious but unsuccessful reclamation work instigated by Sir Henry Calthorpe, a local landowner.

WALK 6
Blakeney and Blakeney Downs

Start/finish	*Blakeney village sign on The Quay*
Locate	*///released.jolt.century*
Cafes/pubs	*Blakeney*
Transport	*Coasthopper CH1 bus service from Cromer and Wells-next-the-Sea*
Parking	*Pay & display car park at Blakeney Quay (NR25 7ND) or free car park at village hall, Langham Road (NR25 7PG)*
Toilets	*Quay and village hall*

Time 1hr 30min
Distance 5.3km (3.3 miles)
Climb 55m

A short but varied walk centred on an attractive coastal village that was once an important fishing port

This short walk, which starts and finishes in the picturesque flint-built village of Blakeney, offers plenty of variety along the way. After taking in a short stretch of saltmarsh, so typical of this part of the north Norfolk coast, it climbs gently inland through the farmland of Blakeney Downs before returning to the village by way of St Nicholas's Church, whose two towers serve as a local landmark.

Looking back to Blakeney from the Norfolk Coast Path

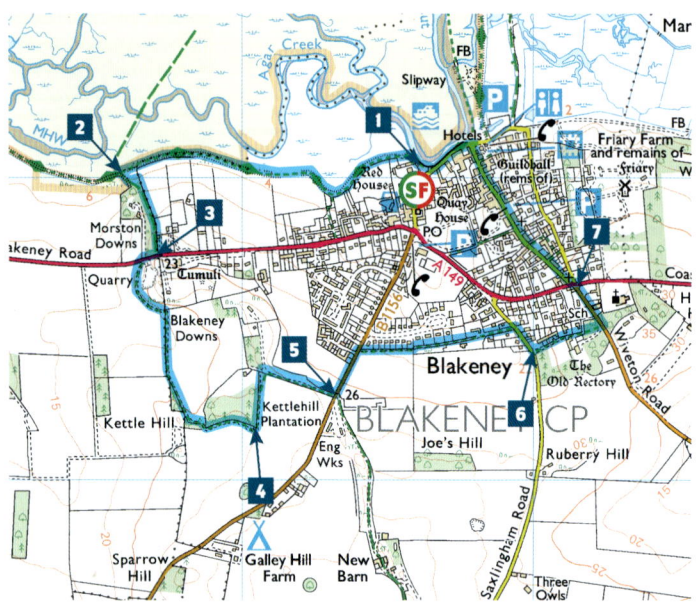

1 From the Blakeney village sign take the path away from The Quay that leads around the back of a flint pebble building. This goes past gardens to follow a raised track beside salt marshes. Continue until reaching a Norfolk Coast Path sign where steps lead left up to another path to the left.

2 Turn left along this narrow path and follow it to soon arrive at the **A149** coast road where there is a Blakeney road sign.

3 Crossing the road carefully, turn right and then almost immediately left along the signed footpath that leads inland. This curves around the base of an isolated hill before reaching a field edge. Continue along the path next to the hedgerow and follow it as it passes a wood and then curves left alongside a wooden fence until the path reaches a sharp left at **Kettlehill Plantation**.

4 Follow the path as it turns sharply left around the corner of Kettlehill Plantation and continue to arrive at a surfaced track. There are excellent views back to the coast from here. Turn right along the track to soon arrive at a road.

5 Turn left and follow the road for a short distance before taking the footpath to the right that leads between fields and gardens. Arriving at another minor road, turn right for a short distance to reach another footpath to the left. The towers of St Nicholas's Church can be seen clearly across the fields ahead.

St Nicholas's Church, Blakeney, with its two towers

6 Take the footpath, which leads left past garden fences, to reach **Wiveton Road**. Turn left to walk downhill past the school and the entrance to the graveyard of **St Nicholas's Church** to reach the main road.

Blakeney's St Nicholas's Church is well worth a short detour. The church is notable for having two towers, the original 13th-century one and a smaller 15th-century addition above the chancel, the purpose of which is uncertain.

7 At the main road, cross carefully to go down High Street, the left-hand option of the two roads opposite. Here you will pass a variety of the flint pebble buildings that characterise many of the villages of the north Norfolk coast. This will soon bring you to the harbour. Turn left along The Quay and go past the Blakeney Hotel to return to the starting point.

The port of Blakeney

Unlike its neighbour Cley next the Sea, whose fortunes declined centuries ago when its harbour silted up, Blakeney remained an active port until as late as the early 20th century, when it too underwent the same fate. At odds with its genteel modern-day image, in the early medieval period Blakeney had a reputation for piracy, and lawless residents who would regularly steal the cargo from boats docked in the harbour. These days only small boats are able make their way to the sea from its harbour and the village remains a firm favourite of the Norfolk yachting set.

A black-headed gull and grain loading gantry at Wells harbour

WALK 7
Wells-next-the-Sea and Holkham

Start/finish	Corner of Freeman Street and Beach Road, Wells-next-the-Sea
Locate	///roadmap.winds.mulls
Cafes/pubs	Pubs and cafes at Wells-next-the-Sea and Holkham
Transport	Buses from Fakenham, Cromer and King's Lynn
Parking	Freeman Street pay & display car park (NR23 1AS)
Toilets	Freeman Street and Beach Road car parks

Time 3hr
Distance 10km (6.2 miles)
Climb 25m

A longer walk, close to the coast, that links the seaside town of Wells-next-the-Sea with the Holkham Estate

This fairly long but rewarding walk has a little bit of everything: a seaside town with harbour, muddy creeks, woodland, grazing farmland and elegant estate parkland. It also provides access to what many describe as one of England's most iconic beaches. While there are a couple of places to stop for refreshments along the way much of this walk also offers opportunities for a leisurely picnic stop and/or a swim en route.

Beach huts near Wells Lifeboat Station

1 Starting at the corner of Freeman Street and Beach Road, go along Beach Road a little way before taking the raised pathway that runs parallel to the road. This gives good views back to Wells harbour and across to Wells Salt Marshes on the other side of the water. Continue along here until you reach a cafe and car park just before **Wells Lifeboat Station**. A Norfolk Coast Path sign points left.

A short detour at this point is to continue past the lifeboat station and go down to the beach, where a line of colourful beach huts on stilts backs onto the pine plantation.

2 Follow the sign to go left, crossing the road down to the **parking area** and cafe with outdoor seating. Head past the cafe to take the signed path ('Norfolk Coast Path: The Lookout Cafe 1¾ miles') that leads straight on alongside a pine plantation. This skirts a lake before continuing for about another 2.5 km along the edge of a pine belt. Follow this until reaching Lady Anne's Drive, where there is a modern-looking **visitor centre** and cafe called the Lookout.

ⓘ Halfway along Lady Anne's Drive is the remains of Holkham railway station, which was closed in 1952.

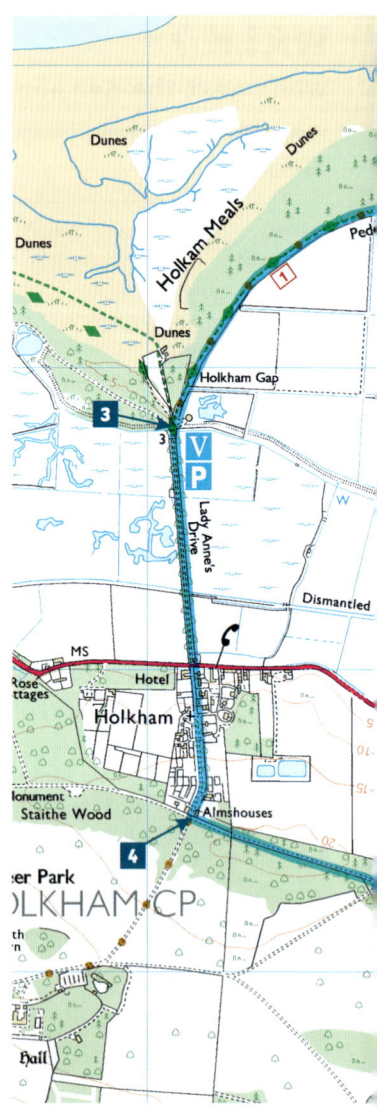

WALK 7 – WELLS-NEXT-THE-SEA AND HOLKHAM

43

A shady stretch of pine plantation on the way to Holkham

With seemingly endless sand at low tide, Holkham Beach is Norfolk's most famous beach. It has been used as a film location on more than one occasion, most notably in *Shakespeare in Love* (1998) and, more recently, *Deadpool & Wolverine* (2024).

3 Turn left along **Lady Anne's Drive** and follow it until it joins the **A149** coast road. Cross the road to head up the main driveway of Holkham Hall as far as an archway next to some **almshouses**.

4 Pass under the archway and then turn left along the path that leads through mixed woodland. Follow this, continuing in the same direction at a crossroads of tracks to arrive at an isolated house, **East Lodge**. Go through the gate to continue along the drive until reaching the **A149** at a corner.

5 Turn immediately right along a farm track, and then left where it reaches a crossroads of tracks. Follow this until coming to a minor road at the edge of Wells.

WALK 7 – WELLS-NEXT-THE-SEA AND HOLKHAM

War Memorial at the Holkham Estate

Holkham Hall

Holkham Hall is an 18th-century country house designed in the Palladian style by the architect William Kent. It was built for Thomas Coke, the 1st Earl of Leicester, although the aristocrat, who died in 1759, did not live to see the work completed in his lifetime. While the house has a fine Marble Hall and opulent state rooms, it is some of the architectural features of the estate itself, like the Triumphal Arch, completed in 1752, and the 30m-high obelisk, which stands at the highest point in the estate, that are more immediately obvious to casual visitors.

Boats at Wells harbour

6 Turn left along the **B1105**, then, almost immediately, turn right into Burnt Street. Follow Burnt Street for a short distance then, just after passing Flint Drive to the right, turn left along a narrow alleyway. This leads to Plummers Hill. Turn left here, passing the open green of the Buttlands and the Crown Hotel before continuing along Chancery Lane to reach High Street. Crossing High Street, continue in the same direction along School Lane to arrive at Polka Road.

7 Turn left along Polka Road to go down to **The Harbour**. Turn left here to pass beneath the loading gantry of a former granary before returning to the starting point on **Beach Road**.

– To shorten

The only way to shorten this walk is to catch a Coastliner 36 bus back to Wells at the entrance to the Holkham Estate on the A149 (between waypoints 3 and 4). This would shorten the walk by about 1hr (although the bus service itself is only hourly).

WALK 8
Burnham Deepdale to Burnham Overy Staithe

Time 2hr
Distance 6.5km (4 miles)
Climb 15m

An easy coastal walk between villages that follows a lovely section of the Norfolk Coast Path

Start	Layby opposite Dalegate Market, Burnham Deepdale
Finish	Burnham Overy Staithe harbour
Locate	///fermented.silks.flexibly
Cafes/pubs	Cafe at Burnham Deepdale, pub at Burnham Overy Staithe
Transport	Coastliner 36 bus service from King's Lynn and Fakenham
Parking	Layby next to St Mary's Church opposite Dalegate Market and at Dalegate Market
Toilets	Burnham Overy Staithe

This one-way walk, which follows a section of the Norfolk Coast Path, connects two contrasting villages in northwest Norfolk. It begins at Burnham Deepdale, which has a wide range of amenities, and ends at Burnham Overy Staithe, a popular boating centre. A regular bus service connects the two villages, but it would be equally rewarding to return by walking the route in reverse.

Following the raised bank between marshes and mudflats

SHORT WALKS NORFOLK

1 Facing the shops and garage of Dalegate Market opposite the layby, turn right and right again along The Drove. Then turn right again at a footpath signed 'Restricted Byway: Norfolk Coast Path 100m', which leads to a footpath along a raised bank. Follow this as it curves gently eastwards with marshes on the right and mudflats on the seaward side until the raised bank makes a sharp right-angled turn to the right.

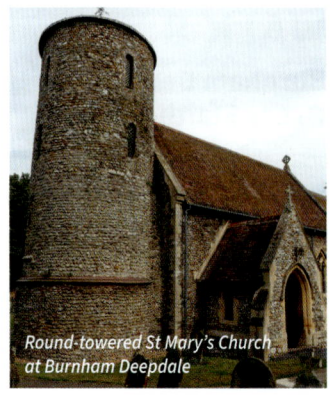

Round-towered St Mary's Church at Burnham Deepdale

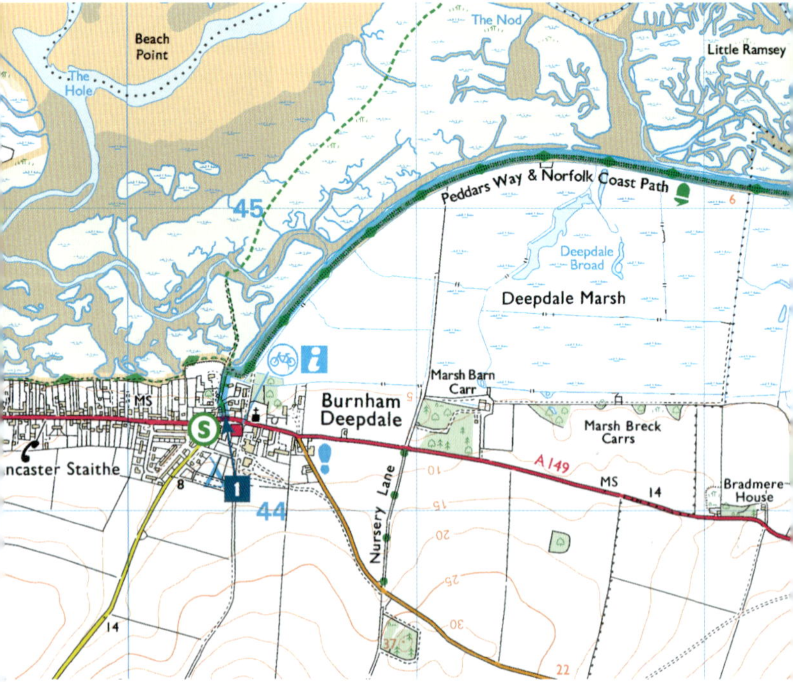

WALK 8 – BURNHAM DEEPDALE TO BURNHAM OVERY STAITHE

Scolt Head Island, Norfolk's most northerly point, can be seen across the channel to the left. An important place for nesting Sandwich terns, the island can be reached in summer by ferry from Brancaster Staithe or Burnham Overy Staithe.

2 Ignore the footpath sign pointing diagonally across a field and follow the raised bank inland alongside a channel until reaching another footpath. Fork left and follow the path over a footbridge towards a black **windmill** ahead. At a crossroads of paths continue ahead to cross a field diagonally to reach the main coast road.

3 Turn left at the road and take the footpath to the left that leads behind a hedge parallel to the road. When this re-emerges on the road continue along the pavement into the village until reaching a Norfolk Coast Path signpost next to a **phone box**.

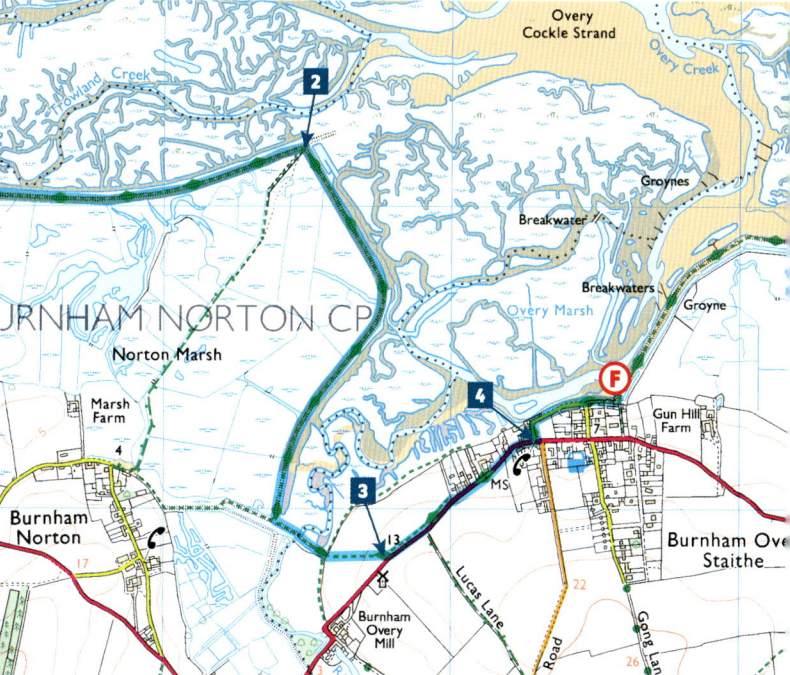

Looking north to Scolt Head Island

The Norfolk Coast Path is a 135km long distance walking trail that follows the coast between Hunstanton and Hopton-on-Sea. For much of the route it passes though the Norfolk Coast Area of Outstanding Natural Beauty (AONB).

4 Turn left and follow the lane around to the right to arrive at **Burnham Overy Staithe** harbour. The harbour is a major centre for recreational sailing and there is a well-provisioned chandlery here in addition to an art gallery. The Hero pub and the stop for the bus back to Burnham Deepdale is just a little way up East Harbour Way to the right.

> ⓘ *Burnham Overy Staithe's pub, the Hero, takes its name from local hero Horatio Nelson, who learned to sail here as a boy.*

WALK 8 – BURNHAM DEEPDALE TO BURNHAM OVERY STAITHE

A view of Burnham Overy Staithe from the Norfolk Coast Path

The Burnhams

A total of six villages with the name Burnham lie within walking distance of each other in the valley of the River Burn in northwest Norfolk. Burnham Deepdale and Burnham Overy Staithe both straddle the coast road, while Burnham Norton and Burnham Market, which now incorporates the parishes of Burnham Westgate and Burnham Ulph, can be found a little way inland to the south, as can Burnham Thorpe, Horatio Nelson's birthplace. Curiously, Burnham Overy Town, with just a few houses to its name, is anything but a town and the smallest by far of all these settlements.

SHORT WALKS NORFOLK

Clockwise from top L: Saltmarshes west of Blakeney (Walk 6); A signpost on the shingle beach at Cley Eye (Walk 5); Sheringham and the Norfolk coast from the top of Beeston Hill (Walk 4); A WWII pillbox in the dunes (Walk 1)

Clockwise from the top: Traditional flint cottages line Blakeney High Street (Walk 6); At the entrance to Cromer Pier (Walk 3); Holy Trinity Church, West Runton (Walk 4); Approaching Wells harbour (Walk 7)

St Mary's Church with its 15th-century tower, Holme-next-the-Sea

WALK 9
Thornham and Holme-next-the-Sea

Time 3hr 30min
Distance 10.7km (6.6 miles)
Climb 50m

A longer route that takes in some of the best of northwest Norfolk: attractive villages, saltmarsh, dunes and beach

Start/finish	All Saints Church, Thornham
Locate	///workbench.tumble.yield
Cafes/pubs	Pubs in Thornham and Holme-next-the-Sea, cafe at Holme Dunes nature reserve
Transport	Coastliner 36 bus from King's Lynn and Fakenham
Parking	On street
Toilets	Holme Dunes nature reserve

This is a longer walk than most but one that is full of interest. Starting at the picturesque village of Thornham, the route skirts reedbeds before joining a section of the Norfolk Coast Path that leads to the beach at Holme Dunes nature reserve. From here, it veers inland through the village of Holme-next-the-Sea before taking a higher route along little-used country lanes to return to the start.

Passing Broad Water on the way to Holme Dunes

SHORT WALKS NORFOLK

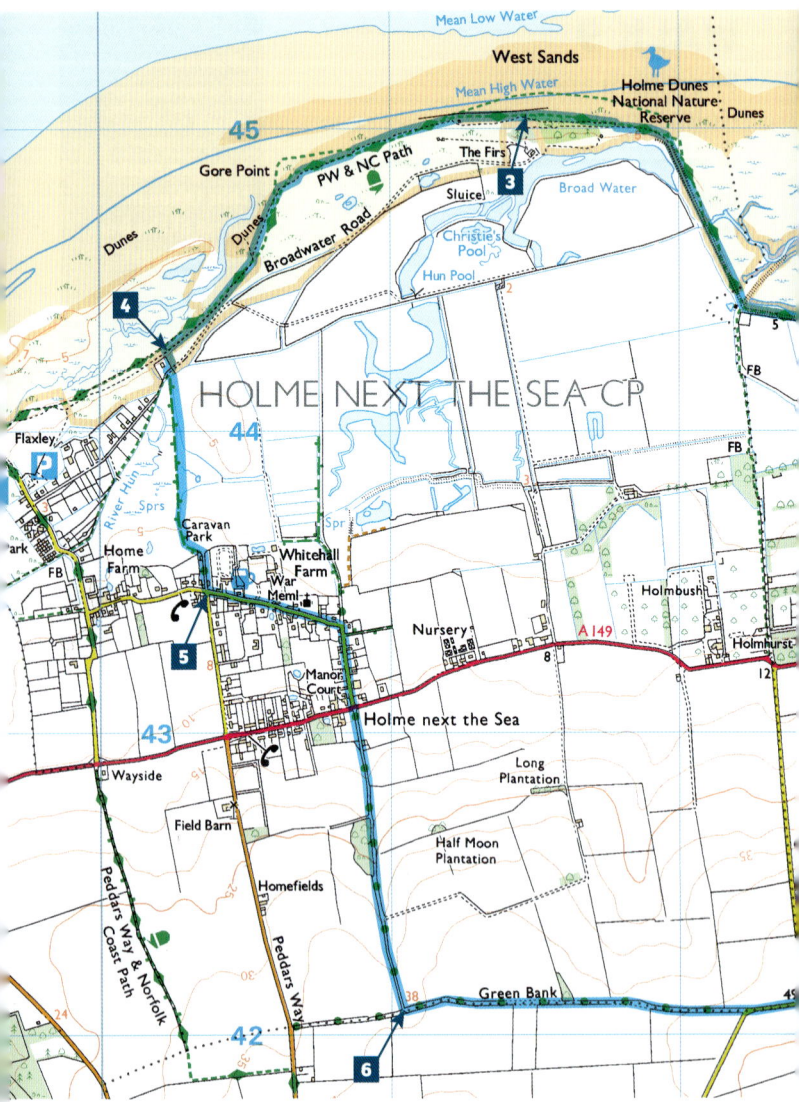

WALK 9 – THORNHAM AND HOLME-NEXT-THE-SEA

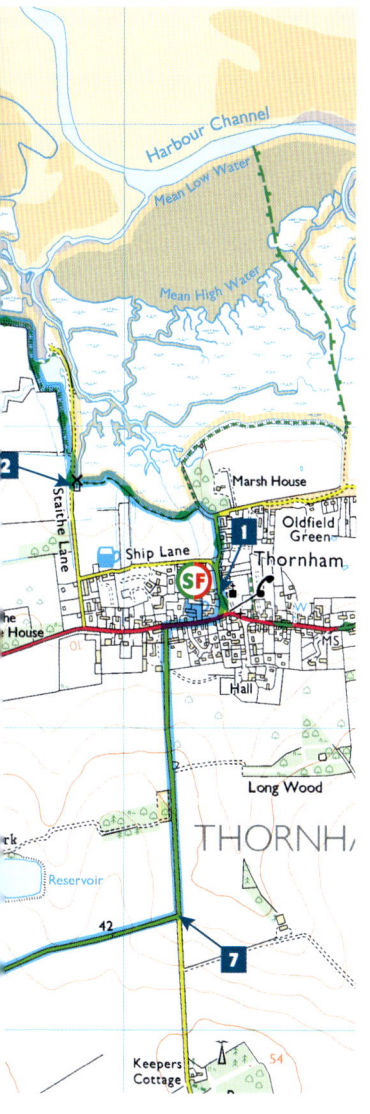

1 With the church entrance gate behind you, turn right to walk down Church Lane past Thornham Manor. Continue past a road to the left to reach an area of woodland where the road curves right. Leave the road here to take the track to the left, which soon arrives at a Norfolk Coast Path signpost. Follow this left over a footbridge through an area of reedbeds and rough grazing until reaching a rough track.

Many of the houses in Thornham and neighbouring villages are built from material unusual elsewhere in Norfolk: white chalk blocks interspersed with a ginger-coloured sandstone called carrstone, which is found locally in this northwest corner of the county.

2 Turn right along the track then climb up to the bank where there is another sign for the Norfolk Coast Path. The raised path goes past a barn to the right before continuing through a wide area of mudflats and tidal channels. The flint, chalk and brick barn, built in the 18th or 19th century was probably built for storing shipped goods like coal. After passing **Broad Water**, a large body of water to the left, the path joins a boardwalk. Ignore the signed path to Holme Bird Observatory to the left and continue through sand

A boardwalk leads to Holme Bird Observatory

dunes and a woodland area. This arrives at a gap in the dunes where a signpost points inland to the Holme Dunes visitor centre (where there is a cafe and toilets) and ahead to the site where Seahenge was discovered.

> **Holme Dunes is a 192-hectare nature reserve located close to where the North Sea meets the Wash. It possesses a variety of habitats that include mudflats, beach, sand dunes, pine woods, freshwater lake and saltmarsh.**

3 From the signpost, continue along the coast path through the dunes, passing a concrete World War 2 pillbox and an information board about Seahenge along the way. Carry on until reaching a small car park just below the path to the left.

4 Go down into the car park and out through the entrance into a lane. Almost immediately, take the footpath to the left that leads through a gate into Redwell Marsh reserve. This passes through meadows to arrive at another gate with a Redwell Marsh

The beach at Holme Dunes

SSSI sign. Go through the gate and follow Bussey's Lane past farm buildings to reach a junction.

5 Turn left, passing the **White Horse pub** and St Mary's Church, then right along East Gate to reach the **A149** coast road. Head straight across and along Chalkpit Lane, a narrow lane that climbs uphill to reach a T-junction.

6 Turn left along **Green Bank**, a quiet minor road. This passes a road to the right and then a crossroads with a triangulation pillar. Continue along Green Bank to descend slightly before reaching another T-junction.

7 Go left, following the road downhill into **Thornham** village. At the High Street, turn right to pass the **Orange Tree** pub to return to the start point by the church.

All Saints Church with its squat square tower, Thornham

– To shorten

The walk can be shortened by taking a bus (hourly) back to Thornham from Holme-next-the-Sea. Instead of going up Chalkpit Lane after Waypoint 5, turn right along the main road to find the bus stop at the next junction. This will shorten the walk by about 3km (1hr).

Seahenge

The early Bronze Age structure known as Seahenge (so-called because of its resemblance to Stonehenge) was discovered in 1998 when an exceptionally low tide at Holme-next-the-Sea revealed a circle of 55 split oak timbers surrounding a large, upturned tree trunk. Carbon dating revealed that the circle, together with another nearby timber circle, was erected in the spring and summer of 2049BCE. Although its function is uncertain, the structure was most probably built for the performance of rituals, and it is possible that the 'henge' provided an enclosure in which dead bodies were laid out on the central upturned stump.

Dappled light on the trail through the woods of Sandringham Royal Parkland

WALK 10
Sandringham Royal Parkland

Start/finish	The Courtyard, Sandringham
Locate	///songbook.umbrella.ankle
Cafes/pubs	Cafe at the Courtyard
Transport	Bus from King's Lynn and Hunstanton
Parking	Two pay & display car parks, North and West (PE35 6AB)
Toilets	In the Courtyard

Time 1hr 30min
Distance 4.5km (2.8 miles)
Climb 30m

An easy, shady woodland walk through Sandringham Royal Parkland

Starting at the Sandringham Courtyard this enjoyable woodland stroll offers an easy route through an attractive country park in northwest Norfolk. There is also the optional bonus of a fleeting glimpse of the Wash that lies at some distance to the west. This walk could be done as either as an outing in its own right or as an addition to a visit to the famous royal residence.

The Courtyard visitor centre, Sandringham

SHORT WALKS NORFOLK

1 Facing away from the buildings of the Courtyard turn right, crossing an access road, to follow a path, signed with a blue and yellow post, that leads to woodland ahead. This soon reaches a signboard that describes two way-marked trails: blue and yellow.

2 Take the path through woodland, passing a large carved wooden bear, to reach a yellow-marked post. Follow this path and go along it until joining a broader path where it rejoins the blue route. Continue along here a short distance to reach a marker post where a minor path diverts off to the right. A short detour along here leads to an observation platform that offers views west across to the open water of the Wash.

3 Continue along the broad path until arriving at a minor road and a pair of gates that commemorate Queen Elizabeth II's Golden Jubilee in 2002.

Sandringham House was first opened to the public in 1977 on the occasion of Queen Elizabeth II's Silver Jubilee. Sandringham Gardens were opened by King Edward VII in 1908.

4 Cross the road and continue through woodland until reaching another road.

A carved wooden bear in the woods

ⓘ *Sandringham House, a royal residence of King Charles III, was rebuilt in the Jacobean style in the late 19th century.*

WALK 10 – SANDRINGHAM ROYAL PARKLAND

5 Just before the road, take the signed (blue post) path to the left, which runs parallel to the road for some distance before reaching another road close to a junction.

6 Cross the road and continue in the same direction, following the woodland path that runs close to the road. This passes a **car park** before emerging from the woods immediately opposite the Courtyard and starting point.

Some areas of Sandringham Royal Parkland have mixed woodland

– To shorten
Follow the blue signs throughout for a shorter 3km (2 mile) walk that should take no longer than 1hr in total.

Sandringham Royal Parkland

The park was created in 1968 when an area of 142 hectares of Queen Elizabeth's Norfolk estate was designated a country park. Sandringham Royal Parkland now comprises 243 hectares. The park has two nature trails in addition to a sculpture trail and 20-point orienteering route. The park, which is planted with a mixture of deciduous and evergreen trees – Corsican and Scots pines, oak, sweet chestnut and birch – is open to the public all year round. Each season has its own charm but a particularly good time to come is in May when the rhododendrons are in bloom.

WALK 11
Historic Norwich

Start/finish	The Forum, Norwich
Locate	///vague.stone.tester
Cafes/pubs	Pubs, cafes and restaurants in Norwich
Transport	Buses from the rest of Norfolk
Parking	The Forum pay & display car park, Bethel Street (NR2 1TF)
Toilets	The Forum

This circuit of central Norwich provides a good introduction to the city's rich history. While it takes in many medieval churches and civic buildings along the way, it starts and ends at Norwich's most iconic modern building, the Forum. For part of the way it follows the Wensum, the river that bisects the city. It also passes the Norman cathedral and Pull's Ferry, where stone for the cathedral was unloaded at a watergate.

Time 1hr 30min
Distance 4.4km (2.7miles)
Climb 25m

Get a sense of Norwich's historic past with this varied, city centre circuit

Cow Tower on River Wensum, Norwich

1 Facing St Peter Mancroft Church opposite the Forum, go left to walk past the front of **City Hall**. Norwich Market, which has been at its present site for 900 years, lies immediately below to the right, beyond which Norwich's Norman castle can be seen on a rise. Go past the top of the elegantly flint-faced Guildhall and continue along Lower Goat Lane. At the end of the lane, take the diagonal path in front of **St Gregory's Church** and continue down the alley to reach St Benedict's Street.

> ⓘ *The Norwich Lanes, home to many independent retailers, is a network of courtyards, alleyways and open spaces between St Giles and St Benedict's Street.*

The 15th-century Guildhall provides a fine example of the flint flushwork that characterises many of the city's medieval churches and civic buildings. The building has been used as a gaol, a court and a seat for local government during its lifetime.

2 Turn left along St Benedict's Street then, immediately past **St Lawrence's Church**, go right down St Lawrence Steps to reach Westwick Street. Crossing the road carefully, continue along Coslany Street to reach a bridge over the river. Carry on a little further before turning right along Colegate, which passes **St Michael Coslany Church** before reaching Duke Street. Cross over and continue along Colegate passing **St George's Church**

Norwich's 15th-century Guildhall with its superb flint flushwork

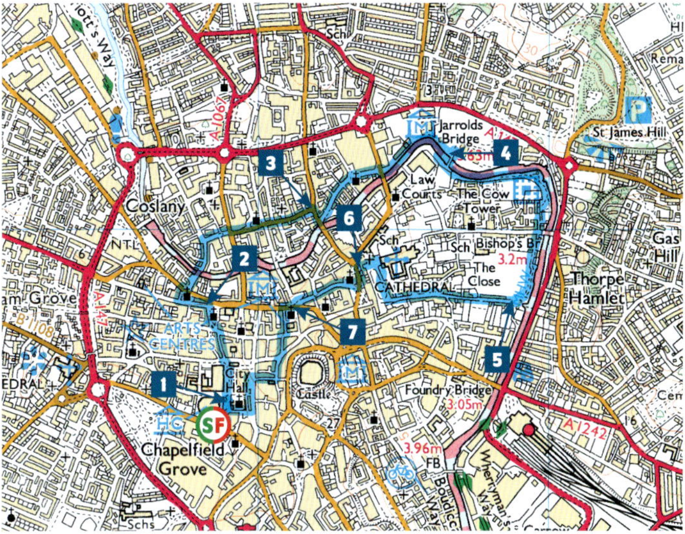

WALK 11 – HISTORIC NORWICH

Jarrolds Bridge over the River Wensum

and an **octagonal chapel** to arrive at Magdalen Street.

3 Turn right, then left along Fishergate to reach Whitefriars. Cross the road and continue in the same direction following the riverside path. This passes St James Mill, a tall Victorian building, before arriving at **Jarrolds Bridge**.

4 Cross the river by the bridge and then turn left, following the riverside path past **Cow Tower**, a medieval artillery tower, until arriving at Bishopgate, where there is a bridge across the river. Cross the road and continue along the river path to reach Pull's Ferry.

Norwich Cathedral has the second highest spire in England

Norwich's medieval churches

It used to be said that Norwich has a pub for every day of the year and a church for every week. If this were ever the case for drinking establishments, it is no longer true as these days Norwich has only around 100 pubs within its outer ring road. It is a different matter for churches though, as at one time there were 57 churches within the city walls. A total of 31 medieval churches still survive, although two-thirds of these are redundant or serving a non-ecclesiastical function.

WALK 11 – HISTORIC NORWICH

Tombland Alley with its crooked medieval buildings

Pull's Ferry, a 15th-century flint building, stands on the spot where Caen stone from Normandy was once transported from the River Wensum to the cathedral construction site. The ferry that used to operate here ceased operation in 1943.

5 Turn right along Ferry Lane and continue to **The Close**. Then, head towards the medieval gate ahead before going right alongside a green towards the cathedral's west door. Turn left in front of **Norwich Cathedral**, leaving the cathedral precinct by Erpingham Gate. To the left of the gate is a statue to Edith Cavell, the World War 1 nurse who was executed by the Germans as a spy.

6 Turn left out of Erpingham Gate to go a little way along Tombland before crossing the road to pass beneath an arch into Tombland Alley. This passes several crooked medieval houses before emerging on Princes Street. Turn right along Princes Street to arrive at St Andrew's Street.

7 Cross the road here, then turn right, then left, to go up Bridewell Alley. Crossing Bedford Street, carry on to reach pedestrianised London Street. Turn right and continue until arriving at the entrance to the Art Nouveau-style Royal Arcade. Go right and walk through the arcade to reach Gentleman's Walk. Turn left and then right next to St Peter Mancroft Church to return to the starting point at the Forum.

A colourful Millennium Milepost at Whitlingham Broad

WALK 12
Whitlingham Country Park

Start/finish	*Whitlingham Great Broad*
Locate	*///dime.moons.comb*
Cafes/pubs	*Cafe at Whitlingham Broad car park*
Transport	*Buses from Norwich to Trowse village, 1km away*
Parking	*Whitlingham Country Park pay & display car park (NR14 8TR)*
Toilets	*In car park*

Time 2hr
Distance 6.2km (3.9 miles)
Climb 40m

An enjoyable waterside and woodland stroll close to Norwich

Whitlingham Country Park on the southern fringe of Norwich is centred upon Whitlingham Great Broad, a manmade lake on the site of a former gravel quarry that has been allowed to regenerate over the past 20 years. The broad, a popular local leisure spot with facilities for water-based activities like rowing and paddle boarding, is a haven for wildlife throughout the year. The route described here circuits the broad before following a loop through mixed woodland.

The flint barn at Whitlingham Broad

SHORT WALKS NORFOLK

1 Starting at the waterside just down from the flint barn, turn left along the path to pass a brightly painted Sustrans Millennium Milepost on the right and the ruins of **Trowse Newton Hall** to the left. Follow the path as it curves to the right around the western end of the Great Broad – with Little Broad to the left – to reach the water activity centre.

> Trowse Newton Hall, now little more than a picturesque ruin, was once known as Millionaires' Row. The 15th-century hall once served as a country retreat for the priors of Norwich Cathedral. Edward III is believed to have once lodged here.

2 Go right at the activity centre to follow the path with the broad to your right. A channel of the River Yare flows beyond the raised bank on the left, a popular stretch of river for canoeists. Passing a wooded peninsula on the right, where there is a sign for a bird hide, continue past **Thorpe Bridge** on the other side of the river to arrive at a point where the path divides just before an area of woodland.

> ⓘ *The River Yare has its confluence with the Wensum, the river that flows through Norwich, just west of Whitlingham Great Broad.*

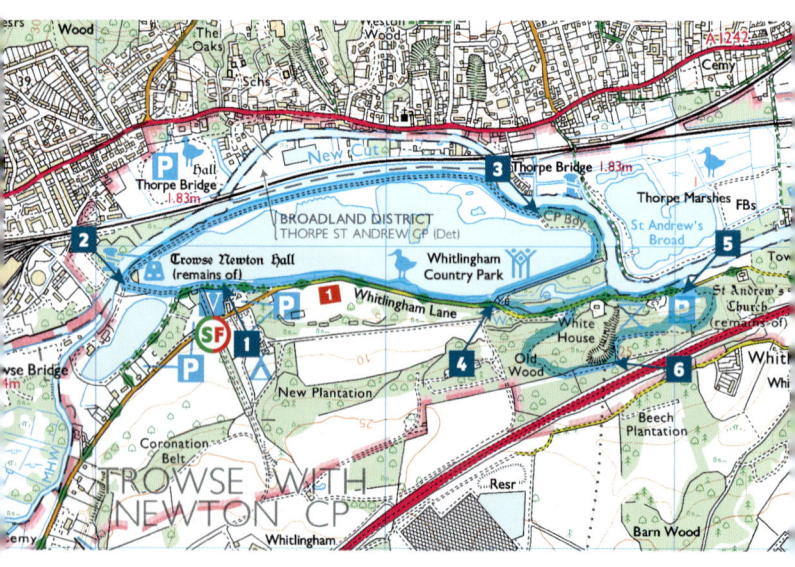

WALK 12 – WHITLINGHAM COUNTRY PARK

Canoeing on Whitlingham Broad

3 Take the left-hand fork that leads alongside the river for a short distance before looping back round through woodland to follow the southern shore of the broad. This section offers views across to St Andrew's Broad and Thorpe Marshes, a nature reserve on the other side of the river. Continue along the south shore of the broad until reaching a path with a 'Dogs on Leads' sign that leads off to the left across a dyke.

4 Take the path to the left, which crosses a meadow before arriving at a road. Turn left at the road, passing a **white house** and a picnic site before reaching a **car park** on the right.

5 At the car park take the 'Woodland Footpath' sign that leads into the woods. Follow the path as it climbs and then levels out onto a broader track between plantations. Continue to reach a flight of wooden steps that lead downhill.

6 Go down the steps and continue along the path as it loops to the right to eventually rejoin the road by the broad. Turn left along the road, retracing steps as far as Waypoint 4 where it rejoins the waterside path around the broad. Turn left to complete the circuit of the broad and return to the starting point by the flint barn.

SHORT WALKS NORFOLK

Descending the steps in Whitlingham Woods

— To shorten

Rather than doing the leg through the woods at Waypoint 4, simply continue along the waterside path at this point to soon return to the start. This will shorten the walk by at least 2km (45min).

Wildlife at Whitlingham Country Park

Whitlingham Country Park was designated a Local Nature Reserve in 2009. The reserve encompasses both Great and Little Broads and the picnic meadow and woodland at the park's eastern end. The Great Broad is a haven for water birds that include herons, cormorants and a variety of ducks, geese and swans. Kingfishers are also occasionally seen, as are otters. Dragonflies and butterflies are plentiful at the water's edge in summer. The trees that line the broad host a good selection of migratory warblers in spring, while woodpeckers and nuthatches may also be seen in the more extensive woodland areas to the east.

WALK 13
Great Yarmouth

Start/finish	*Great Yarmouth Minster*
Locate	*///gaps.storm.tummy*
Cafes/pubs	*Pubs and cafes in Great Yarmouth*
Transport	*Trains and buses from Norwich*
Parking	*Market Place pay & display car park (NR30 1LX) or Brewery Plain pay & display car park (NR30 1PL)*
Toilets	*North Drive near Britannia Pier*

Time 2hr
Distance 5.9km (3.7 miles)
Climb 5m

Great Yarmouth beyond the beach – ancient walls, medieval buildings and a historic seafaring tradition

This amble around Norfolk's largest seaside town focuses on Great Yarmouth's historical side, in particular its long-held seafaring tradition. Starting at Great Yarmouth Minster (St Nicholas'), the town's most important church, it follows a section of medieval town wall before emerging on South Quay. From here it follows a meandering route back to the seafront, where Yarmouth's more familiar side as a popular seaside resort can be clearly seen.

Britannia Pier, one of Yarmouth's two piers

1 Facing away from Great Yarmouth Minster's entrance gate, walk up Church Plain past Anna Sewell House and cross Priory Plain at the traffic lights. Continue along Church Plain past the entrance to the **Fishermen's Hospital** and the wooden Market Hall. Keep going along Market Place, crossing Regent Road and continuing in the same direction along Dene Side to reach Alexandra Road.

ⓘ *The Fishermen's Hospital, built in 1702 to house retired fishermen and their wives, is a historic almshouse originally consisting of 20 individual cottages.*

2 Turn left, then right along St George's Road and then, almost immediately, right again along St Peter's

WALK 13 – GREAT YARMOUTH

A complete section of medieval town wall on Blackfriars' Road

Plain. Reaching St Peter's Road, where there is a large **Greek Orthodox Church**, St Spyridon, cross to continue in the same direction along Blackfriars' Road. A continuous section of medieval town wall runs parallel to the road here. Continue past the entrance to the **Time and Tide Museum** on the left to where Alma Road crosses Blackfriars' Road.

> The Time and Tide Museum of Great Yarmouth Life occupies the Victorian premises of a former herring curing works. The museum tells the story of the town from its ice age origins until the present day.

3 Turn right along Alma Road, then left along Trinity Place to reach Friars' Lane. Go left here to reach South Quay.

4 At South Quay, turn right to walk along the river footpath until reaching a bridge. Cross the road here and continue as far as a roundabout in front of the imposing Victorian Town Hall. Go across the roundabout and carry on in the same direction, passing an isolated flint and brick tower to the left. This is North West Tower, which stood at the most northerly point along Yarmouth's medieval town wall. Continue until you reach Rampart Road

Great Yarmouth's St Nicholas' Church was designated a Minster in 2011.

WALK 13 – GREAT YARMOUTH

Great Yarmouth Town Hall

5 Turn right along Rampart Road then, at Northgate Road, go left and then right along Town Wall Road. Turn left at the next junction following the road round to the right before turning left along West Road. Follow this as it curves right before turning left at the next junction to arrive at Kitchener Road. Turn right to follow the road that divides two parts of a **cemetery**. Cross North Denes Road and continue along Sandown Road to arrive at North Drive close to the beach. To the left is the southern end of the Venetian Waterways, a leisure park with canals, a network of bridges, gardens and a boating lake.

6 Cross over North Drive to reach the seaside promenade. Turn right and follow this as far as the entrance to **Britannia Pier**. At the pier, cross Marine Parade and then go right for a short distance before turning left along Prince's Road. After crossing Nelson Road North, go right along Manby Road and follow this, crossing Euston Road, until just after Tottenham Street on the right, a footpath leads left through a park.

> ⓘ Great Yarmouth has two piers: Britannia Pier and Wellington Pier. Both piers were originally constructed in the 19th century but have been redeveloped many times since.

7 Take the footpath and walk through the park to emerge at the churchyard of **Great Yarmouth Minster**. Walk around the church to return to the start point at the entrance gate.

> **— To shorten**
>
> Turn right at the roundabout just before Waypoint 5 and walk along Fuller's Hill until reaching the entrance to Yarmouth Minster and the start point at Waypoint 1. This will shorten the walk by about 2.5km (45min).

Blackfriars' Tower, one of several that survive in Yarmouth's town walls

Great Yarmouth's town wall

After York, Great Yarmouth has the best-preserved medieval town wall in England. Permission to construct the wall was granted by King Henry III in 1261, although work did not start until 1285. While the main part was completed by 1346, construction continued until around 1400. The wall, which was around 2.5km long and 7m high, was built to enclose the town on three sides, the fourth side being defended by the natural barrier provided by the River Yare. The wall originally had 10 gates along its length in addition to 16 defensive towers, 11 of which survive.

WALK 14
Womack Water and Horse Fen

Start/finish	*Womack Staithe, Ludham*
Locate	*///shadows.eyebrows.hospitals*
Cafes/pubs	*Cafe at Womack Staithe, pub in Ludham*
Transport	*Two-hourly daytime bus service from Norwich*
Parking	*Free parking at Womack Staithe (NR29 5QG)*
Toilets	*Womack Staithe*

Time 1hr 45min
Distance 5.3km (3.3 miles)
Climb 10m

An atmospheric river and fen walk through classic Norfolk Broads scenery close to the village of Ludham

This walk takes in a range of the scenery that is so typical of the Norfolk Broads – water, fen and windmills. Starting and ending at a staithe close to the village of Ludham, it traces the course of a minor boating channel before following the River Thurne, one of the principal waterways of the Broads, for a while. Leaving the river, it loops through fen and woodland on its return to the staithe.

Following the bank of the River Thurne

The derelict Womack Water Drainage Mill can be seen across Horse Fen

WALK 14 – WOMACK WATER AND HORSE FEN

1 With your back to the cafe and shop at Womack Staithe go straight ahead down **Horsefen Road** to pass a toilet block and cottages. Continue past the entrance to the Norfolk Wherry Trust and a couple of **boat yards** on the right. Immediately past Hunter's Yard, take the footpath to the right (the sign may be partially obscured by vegetation), which will soon bring you to **Womack Water**.

2 Turn left along Womack Water and continue along the bank to reach the **River Thurne**, where there is a cottage at the confluence. Turn left to continue along the path next to the river with Horse Fen to your left, where the derelict **Womack Water Drainage Mill** is clearly visible in the middle of the fen. The red-brick, formerly wind-powered three-storey mill has stood without sails for many years.

The Norfolk Broads once had hundreds of working drainage windmills. Many can still be seen in various states of repair today – the largest concentration of windmills in Britain. These were largely replaced by coal-powered mills in the 19th century.

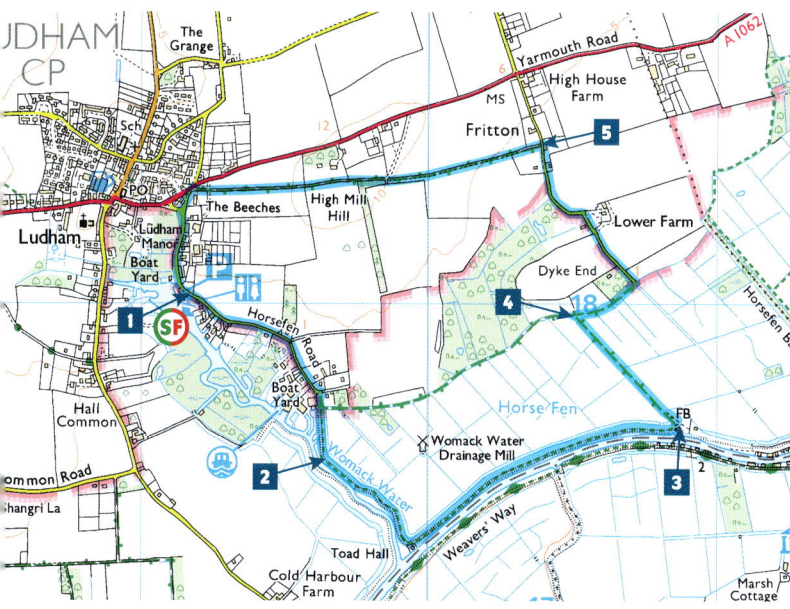

Continue along the riverside path to arrive at Horse Fen pumping station, a small redbrick building.

> ⓘ *The River Thurne, which is just 11km long, is navigable for most of its length.*

3 Turn left over a **footbridge** before taking the broad farm track to the left that leads between large expanses of open fen to reach a gate.

4 Turn right at the gate and follow the track as it turns left at the corner of an area of woodland. Continue along the hedged lane past **Lower Farm** and more woodland to the left to reach a large, partially thatched cottage.

5 Go left along the public bridleway opposite the cottage that leads through woodland and along a field edge and green lane. This crosses another track just before reaching a main road. At the main road, take the short cut to the left to join **Horsefen Road**, which leads left past a converted maltings to return you to the starting point at Womack Staithe.

A sailing boat on the River Thurne

– To shorten

An alternative at Waypoint 4 is to turn left along the track that leads between Horse Fen and woodland to rejoin Horsefen Road next to the boatyard. Turn right here to return to Womack Staithe. This will shorten the walk by about 0.7km (15min).

WALK 14 – WOMACK WATER AND HORSE FEN

The farm track across Horse Fen

The Norfolk Wherry

The Norfolk Wherry is a cargo boat unique to the Broads. Shallow-bottomed and with a collapsible mast giving the ability to pass under bridges, this boat was once used to ferry goods around the broads and rivers of Norfolk and Suffolk. In steep decline by the 1940s, only a few examples remain today. The fully restored 18m-long Albion, which once hauled coal along the River Waveney between the Suffolk towns of Bungay and Lowestoft, is now based at Womack Water in the ownership of the Norfolk Wherry Trust. With its distinctive black sail, it can occasionally be seen plying the waters around Ludham.

Palmer's Drainage Mill at Upton Fen is just one of several windmills in the area

WALK 15
Upton Dyke

Time 1hr 30min
Distance 4.6km (2.9 miles)
Climb 5m

A short but varied walk through typical Broads scenery that takes in river, fen and village

Start/finish	*Upton Dyke*
Locate	*///consoles.divider.sideburns*
Cafes/pubs	*Pub in Upton, also community shop with drinks and snacks*
Transport	*Buses to Acle, 2km away*
Parking	*Upton Dyke free car park (NR13 6BL)*
Toilets	*None on route*

Upton Dyke is actually a staithe (a channel for boat moorings) that leads onto the River Bure, one of the principal rivers of the Norfolk Broads. This short but enjoyable walk begins alongside the staithe before joining the Bure for a while. Heading away from the river it passes through woodland to reach Upton village, where there is a community pub. From here, it follows part of Upton Fen before arriving back at the starting point.

Following the footpath to Upton village

1 From the end of **Upton Dyke** follow the line of boats along the right-hand side of the staithe to soon reach the **River Bure**, where the path curves to the right past **Clippesby Drainage Mill** on the opposite bank. Continue along the river bank until reaching a sign for Northern Rivers Sailing Club and a footpath to the right signed 'Circular Walk, Acle'.

> ⓘ *Palmer's Drainage Mill at the top of Upton Dyke is a rare example of a hollow post windpump, one of only three in the county.*

Five different windmills, typical of the Broads, can be seen on this walk: Palmer's Drainage Mill by Upton Dyke, Clippesby Mill alongside the Bure, Upton Mill and Oby Mill further away to the north, and Fleggburgh Mill to the east.

2 Take the footpath to the right. Reaching a gate, go through it to continue beside a meadow to arrive at another gate that leads through oak woodland alongside a stream. This crosses a footbridge to emerge at a farm track, where a footpath sign points straight ahead.

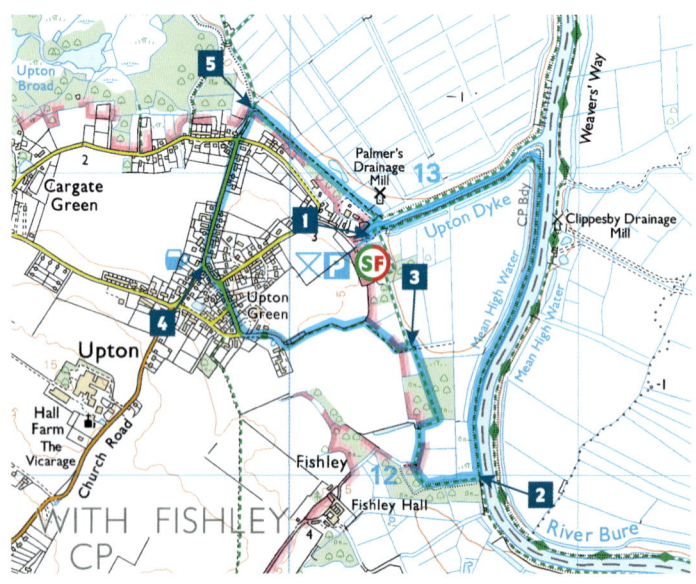

WALK 15 – UPTON DYKE

Horses graze close to Upton Fen

3 Rather than taking the footpath ahead, turn left along the track, which curves left before reaching some farm buildings at Horses Head. Continue past a care home; then take the first road to the right that will bring you to the **White Horse pub** and the shop next door. The pub has been run as a community enterprise since 2012.

4 Turn right at the pub and follow Marsh Road through the village to reach a crossroads. Continue along the rough track opposite; then go through a gate and over a cattle grid until reaching Upton Fen and a footbridge.

Upton Fen is a nature reserve managed by the Norfolk Wildlife Trust. As well as the rare swallow-tail butterfly, its fen, reedbed and grazing marshes provides ideal habitat for many species of dragonfly like the Norfolk hawker.

5 Cross the footbridge and follow the footpath to the right along the edge of the grazing meadows of the fen. This may be a little overgrown in places or wet after rain (an alternative is to turn right at the Marsh Road crossroads and take the road instead). Pass the windmill to the left to arrive back at **Upton Dyke** and the start point by the car park.

The end of the staithe at Upton Dyke

WALK 15 – UPTON DYKE

> ### – To shorten
> At Waypoint 3, instead of taking the track to the left into Upton, continue in the same directions along the signed footpath. This avoids the village and leads directly back to Upton Dyke, shortening the walk by at least 1.5km (30min).

The River Bure

The Bure is the longest river in the Broads and the fourth longest in Norfolk. It rises near Melton Constable in north Norfolk and flows into the North Sea at Gorleston after joining the Yare and Waveney at Breydon Water near Great Yarmouth. Its main tributaries are the Ant and Thurne, the latter a popular river for pleasure boating. The Bure has been navigable as far inland as Horstead Mill near Coltishall since the late 17th century, making the river an important channel for transporting goods like coal, grain and timber to and from the coast.

Along the bank of the River Bure

Clockwise from the top: Pull's Ferry, a former watergate where stone for the cathedral was offloaded (Walk 11); Heading into Whitlingham Woods (Walk 12); The Time and Tide Museum in Great Yarmouth occupies a former herring curing works (Walk 13); A flint wall and hollyhocks line a narrow loke in Cley-next-the-Sea (Walk 5)

Clockwise from top L: One-time fishermen's cottages line a narrow loke in Blakeney (Walk 6); A former maltings at Womack Water (Walk 14); Crossing the Peddars Way in Holme-next-the-Sea (Walk 9); The Hotel de Paris and terraced walkway down to Cromer Pier (Walk 3)

USEFUL INFORMATION

Tourism bodies

Norfolk Broads
www.norfolkbroads.com

Visit the Broads National Park
www.visitthebroads.co.uk

Visit Norfolk
www.visitnorfolk.co.uk

Visit North Norfolk
www.visitnorthnorfolk.com

Visit West Norfolk
www.visitwestnorfolk.com

Tourist information centres

North Norfolk Visitor Centre
Louden Rd, Cromer
www.visitnorthnorfolk.com

Wells-next-the-Sea Visitor Centre
Staithe St, Wells-next-the-Sea
www.visitnorthnorfolk.com

Deepdale Visitor Centre, Deepdale Farm, Burnham Deepdale
www.deepdalecamping.co.uk/information-centre

Travel

Bus
Coasthopper CH
www.sanderscoaches.com

Coastliner 36
www.lynxbus.co.uk

Rail
Greater Anglia
www.greateranglia.co.uk

Great Northern
www.greatnorthernrail.com

East Midlands Railway
www.eastmidlandsrailway.co.uk